79415   3.3

First Facts™

From Farm to Table

From Oranges to Orange Juice

by Kristin Thoennes Keller

Consultant:
Melinda Goodman, Executive Director
TexaSweet Citrus Marketing, Inc.
Mission, Texas

Capstone
press
Mankato, Minnesota

First Facts is published by Capstone Press
151 Good Counsel Drive, P.O. Box 669, Mankato, Minnesota 56002
www.capstonepress.com

Library of Congress Cataloging-in-Publication Data
Thoennes Keller, Kristin.
    From oranges to orange juice / by Kristin Thoennes Keller.
    p. cm.—(First facts. From farm to table)
    Includes bibliographical references and index.
    ISBN 0-7368-2636-X (hardcover)
    1. Orange juice—Juvenile literature. 2. Oranges—Juvenile literature. [1. Orange juice.
2. Oranges.] I. Title. II. Series.
TP441.C5T48 2005
641.8′75—dc22   2003023373

Summary: An introduction to the basic concepts of food production, distribution, and consumption
    by tracing the production of orange juice from oranges to the finished product.

Editorial Credits
Roberta Schmidt, editor; Jennifer Bergstrom, designer; Kelly Garvin, photo researcher; Eric Kudalis,
    product planning editor

Photo Credits
Capstone Press/Gary Sundermeyer, front cover, 5, 19
Comstock Inc., 1
Corbis/Richard T. Nowitz, 11; Royalty-Free, 16–17
Corbis Sygma/Amet Jean Pierre, 20
Grant Heilman Photography/Thomas Hovland, 12–13
Lynn M. Stone, 6–7, 8, 10
PhotoDisc Inc., back cover
Richard T. Nowitz, 14–15
Visuals Unlimited/Inga Spence, 9

1 2 3 4 5 6 09 08 07 06 05 04

Table of Contents

Tasty Orange Juice

Orange juice is a healthy, sweet drink. Some kinds of orange juice have pieces of orange in the juice. These pieces are called pulp. Orange juice sometimes is mixed with other fruit juices.

Orange juice has to be made before people can drink it. Making orange juice takes many steps.

Fun Fact!
Explorer Christopher Columbus brought the first oranges to the Americas more than 500 years ago.

Growing Oranges

Orange juice is made from oranges. Oranges grow on trees. Orange trees grow in warm, sunny places. The trees grow best in sandy dirt. Cool night air makes the fruit a bright orange color. A group of orange trees is called an **orange grove**.

Fun Fact!
An orange can be green and still be ready to eat.

Picking Oranges

Workers often climb ladders to pick oranges. Some kinds of oranges are ready to pick during the winter. Other oranges are picked in the spring.

Workers put the oranges in large
bags on their shoulders. Full bags are
gently dumped into large boxes. Trucks
take the boxes to **packinghouses**.

Packing Oranges

At the packinghouses, machines and people sort and wash the fruit. Some oranges are sold to grocery stores to be eaten fresh.

Oranges also are sold to orange juice makers. Trucks take these oranges to **factories**.

MUCHO
CUIDADO

Desconecte y cierre con
candado el interruptor
eléctrico antes de abrir
las cubiertas.

WARNING

Lock-out electrical
disconnect before
opening covers.

12

Orange Juice

At the factories, machines squeeze the juice out of the oranges. The juice might be heated to kill **germs**.

Machines take water out of much of the juice. A thick, strong syrup is left over. This syrup is called **concentrate**. It is kept in large tanks.

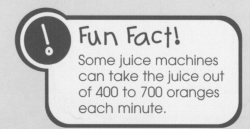

! Fun Fact!
Some juice machines can take the juice out of 400 to 700 oranges each minute.

13

Juice to Drink

Companies buy the orange juice concentrate. Some companies make it into juice for drinking. Workers and machines add water to the concentrate. Sugar or other fruit juices sometimes are added to the orange juice.

Fun Fact!
Parts of oranges are used to make perfume, makeup, soap, bug spray, and paint.

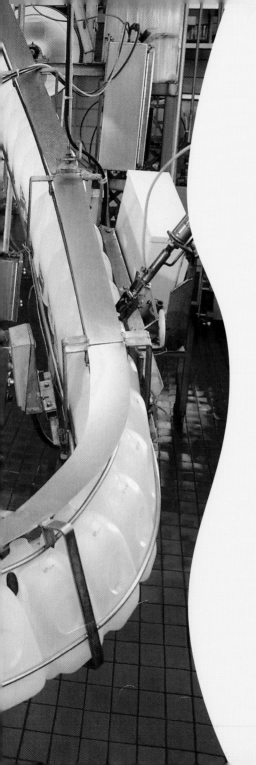

To the Store

The orange juice is put into bottles, **cartons**, or juice boxes. Sometimes, concentrate is put into tubes and frozen.

Companies sell the orange juice to stores. Workers put the orange juice on cold trucks for the trip to the stores.

Where to Find Orange Juice

Orange juice can be found in many places. Grocery stores, gas stations, and many other stores sell orange juice. People can make it at home from concentrate. People can also make orange juice by squeezing fresh oranges.

Fun Fact!
More than half the juice people in the United States drink is orange juice.

Amazing but True!

People in Menton, France, build **sculptures** out of oranges and lemons. Menton's warm, sunny weather makes it a good place to grow these fruits. Every year in February, the people celebrate the orange and lemon crops. Millions of people visit the town to see the amazing sculptures.

Hands On: Orange Ice Pops

You can use orange juice to make a healthy snack. Follow these steps to make ice pops out of orange juice.

What You Need

carton of orange juice
small paper cups
plastic spoons

What You Do

1. Pour the orange juice into the cups. Fill the cups about three-quarters full.
2. Put a plastic spoon in each of the cups. Place the cups in a freezer.
3. Wait for the juice to freeze completely. It will probably take four to five hours. You could leave the cups in the freezer overnight and serve the treats the next day.
4. When the ice pops are ready, tear off the paper cups and eat your frozen treats.

Glossary

carton (KAR-tuhn)—a cardboard or plastic container used for holding or shipping goods

concentrate (KON-suhn-trate)—a thick, strong syrup made by removing water from juice

factory (FAK-tuh-ree)—a building where products are made in large numbers; factories often use machines to make products.

germs (JURMS)—small living things that can cause sickness

orange grove (OR-inj GROHV)—a group of orange trees

packinghouse (PAK-ing-houss)—a building where oranges are washed and packed to be sold

sculpture (SKUHLP-chur)—something shaped out of stone, metal, or another material

Read More

Mayo, Gretchen Will. *Orange Juice.* Where Does Our Food Come From? Milwaukee: Weekly Reader Early Learning Library, 2004.

Snyder, Inez. *Oranges to Orange Juice.* How Things Are Made. New York: Children's Press, 2003.

Spilsbury, Louise. *Oranges.* Food. Chicago: Heinemann Library, 2003.

Internet Sites

FactHound offers a safe, fun way to find Internet sites related to this book. All of the sites on FactHound have been researched by our staff.

Here's how:
1. Visit *www.facthound.com*
2. Type in this special code **073682636X** for age-appropriate sites. Or enter a search word related to this book for a more general search.
3. Click on the **Fetch It** button.

FactHound will fetch the best sites for you!

Index